THORA HIRD'S PRAISE BE!
BOOK OF PRAYERS

D0608489

THORA HIRD'S

Praise Be!

BOOK OF PRAYERS

✳

By Thora Hird
with Elizabeth Gort

Fount
An Imprint of HarperCollinsPublishers

Fount Paperbacks is an Imprint of
HarperCollins*Religious*,
Part of HarperCollins*Publishers*,
77–85 Fulham Palace Road,
Hammersmith, London W6 8JB

First published in Great Britain
in 1992 by Fount Paperbacks

1 3 5 7 9 10 8 6 4 2

Copyright © 1992 Thora Hird and Elizabeth Gort

The Authors assert the moral right to
be identified as the authors of this work

A catalogue record for this book is
available from the British Library

ISBN 0 00 627613-X

Printed and bound in Great Britain by
HarperCollinsManufacturing, Glasgow

Contents

✻

Introduction

✳

I'm just getting ready for our – can you believe it? – *sixteenth* season of *Praise Be!* As usual your letters are flooding in, telling me all about your favourite hymns; I open some of them, and a little poem or prayer falls out of the fold of the paper. They are often words you've written yourselves, and some have even been beautifully printed on cards or in little booklets, to circulate to your friends. And some of them are words you have just come across somewhere, and found helpful, and copied them out because you wanted to share them with your fellow *Praise Be!* viewers. You can't know how much pleasure they give me.

So many of the letters also tell me about troubles – perhaps a mother, father, wife, husband or child who is very ill, so then, when I write back, I say, "I'll put them in my prayers for you" – and I always do.

I've said my prayers kneeling by my bed every night ever since I can remember, since my mother taught me as a tiny girl. At *Praise Be!* time each year the list of people I need to mention to the Lord can get very long, and sometimes I say, "Please excuse me if I don't finish this tonight, as I think I'm going to fall asleep. Do you mind if I come back to you in the morning?" And I never forget. I might just get as far as swinging my legs over the side, but I'll suddenly think: "I've still got some more prayers to do." So I don't get up until I've finished.

(Yes, well – I don't actually kneel beside the bed any longer – I say them *in* bed. But I'm sure the Lord is very understanding about someone with arthritic knees, aren't you?)

Now please don't think that I'm trying to do the vicar's job for him, or to be a clever clogs who can tell you anything you don't already know about praying – in fact it's more the other way around – it's *you* who have taught me so much. But since between us we seem to have been making so many prayers, I thought it would be nice if we had our own *Praise Be! Book of Prayers*.

As I write this, it is still only January, but by the time you are reading it, our sixteenth *Praise Be!* series will be well underway (D.V.), and I'll be coming into your homes on Sunday evenings to read aloud some of these lovable letters I've got in front of me now. So here it is! Your prayers and mine in a little volume which I hope will remind you of all our happy, prayerful years together on *Praise Be!*

January 1992   THORA HIRD

Come, my soul, thy suit prepare;
Jesus loves to answer prayer;
He Himself has bid thee pray,
Therefore will not say thee nay.

Thou art coming to a King,
Large petitions with thee bring;
For His grace and power are such,
None can ever ask too much.

John Newton

Prayers at Bedtime

*

Matthew, Mark, Luke and John,
Bless the bed that I lie on.
Four corners to my bed,
Four angels round my head,
One to watch, and one to pray,
And two to bear my soul away.

Anon

Once upon a time I think nearly all Christians knelt by their bed to say their prayers each night – not just children. It was what most people quite naturally did. I'm sure there are many who still do, but I don't think it's a regular habit with most people any longer. And I wonder how many parents today pray with their children, as well as reading them a bedtime story?

Children don't always pray for quite the right things. I can still remember my prayer when I was about five, and what it was about.

I was born in 1911, and although I think I am quite good at figures, try as I might I cannot make my age any less than eighty years! However, as you will gather, I was three years old when the Great War started (so no one can blame me for starting it!). At that time the toy shops were all selling toy versions of things being used in the war – pretend guns and such like – and amongst the merchandise was a nurse's apron and a proper little three-cornered headpiece, both made in white cotton with a red cross stitched on the front, pinned on a piece of white cardboard, perhaps sixteen inches long by eight inches wide, and sold for a shilling. I don't think I've ever owned anything that gave me more pleasure!

And I will admit that this is what I said in my prayers:

Gentle Jesus, meek and mild,
Look upon a little child;
Pity my simplicity,
Suffer me to come to Thee.

Please bless my Mother and Father
and my sister, Olga, who is with you in heaven,
and my brother, Neville,
And please, God, let the war keep on –
so I can be a nurse and
wear my nurse's uniform. Amen.

What an admission, isn't it? I know you will understand that I had no thought of people killing each other or dying. That didn't enter my five-year-old mind. My mother explained very gently, and asked me to stop saying the "war bit", so I did. As she said, "You have lots of dolls and stuffed animals that you can cure, and you can wear your nurse's uniform whilst you attend them." Aren't mothers wonderful?

Like most children, I had a favourite teddy bear. He'd rather been "in the Wars" himself (if you'll pardon the expression), having lost an eye, which had been replaced with a brown shoe button. (Do any of you remember the little domed shoe buttons we had, in brown or black, on our boots and shoes? No! You're all far too young!) Teddy's other eye was the one he was born – or at any rate, bought – with, a proper toy imitation eye. Matched up with a brown domed shoe button, it gave him a terrible squint! But I didn't care, I loved him dearly. He also had new pads on his paws, better than the original flannel ones. My dearest Mother performed that operation, by cutting the good bits out of a pair of worn out brown leather kid gloves.

But once I had my nurse's uniform, I was impatient to become a fully fledged surgeon myself. I had heard a neighbour telling my mother about an appendix operation. I can still see the look on her face as she lowered her voice to say dramatically, "Of course, they've had to cut her open!"

Wearing my red-cross nurse's uniform, I carefully cut squinting Teddy open with some scissors. The sawdust flew out all over the floor. Poor Ted!

My understanding Mother suggested we got *all* the sawdust out, which we did, leaving a padded head and arms and legs, but a body like an empty paper bag, do you follow? Then she suggested we fill him up with clean linen, and producing a pillow case that had seen better days and had been put on one side for bandages, she helped me to pack it tightly into his body. It was a big success, and Surgeon Mother sewed him up. I laid him in my doll's cot very gently, and was assured by my wonderful Mother that he should be fit and well after dinner, but now we would clear up all the sawdust off the pegged rug!

Well, after that pleasant little wander down memory lane, here are some verses and prayers for last thing at night, before you all go off to sleep with *your* favourite teddies! Our hymn books, too, can provide beautiful night-time thoughts:

> The duteous day now closeth,
> Each flower and tree reposeth,
> Shade creeps o'er wild and wood:
> Let us, as night is falling,
> On God our Maker calling,
> Give thanks to him, the giver good.
>
> Now all the heavenly splendour
> Breaks forth in starlight tender
> From myriad worlds unknown;
> And man, the marvel seeing,
> Forgets his selfish being,
> For joy of beauty not his own.
>
> from the Yattendon Hymnal

May He support us all the day long, till the shadows lengthen, and the evening comes, and the busy world is hushed, and the fever of life over, and our work is done. Then in His mercy, may He give us a safe lodging, and a holy rest, and peace at the last.   Cardinal John Newman

The eternal God is thy refuge, and under-
neath are the everlasting arms.

Deuteronomy 33:27

Lighten our darkness, we beseech thee, O
Lord; and by thy great mercy defend us
from all perils and dangers of this night; for
the love of thy only Son, our Saviour Jesus
Christ.   BCP

Let nothing disturb thee,
Nothing affright thee,
All things are passing,
God never changeth;
Patience endureth,
Attaineth to all things;
Who God possesseth
In nothing is wanting.
Alone God sufficeth.

St Teresa's Bookmark

Be present, O Merciful God, and protect us
through the silent hours of this night, so
that we who are fatigued by the changes
and chances of this fleeting world, may
repose upon thy eternal changelessness.

Leonine Sacramentary, 5th Century

Preserve us, O Lord, while waking,
and guard us while sleeping,
that awake we may watch with Christ,
and asleep we may rest in peace.

Night Prayers

"I have told you these things, so that in me
you may have peace. In this world you will
have trouble. But take heart! I have overcome the world."   John 16:33 (NIV)

Help!

*

There's an old rhyme that runs:

> When in trouble or in doubt
> Wave your arms and rush about!

But most of us pray. Yes, well, of course I know that not everybody prays regularly. I've even heard people say they would like to pray more often, but don't know how. However, in dire emergency, or when life has just knocked you for six, nearly everyone prays. You don't have to be a "Holy Willie" to come to desperate moments when you say, "Please, God, help!" But believers know that the Lord intends us to learn something new from every situation, so he doesn't always answer prayers in the way we expect, or think we want.

I love the imaginary story Rabbi Lionel Blue, who teaches so much while still making us laugh, tells – about a man who has fallen over the edge of a cliff, and is hanging on to a little bush for dear life. This man is an atheist, but in his terror he calls out, "If there is Anyone up there, please save me!"

A great booming voice answers, "Yes, my son. I am here. Have faith. Let go of the bush, and I will lift you safely up in the palm of my hand."

There's a long pause, then the man says, "Is there Anybody *Else* up there?"

Wouldn't it be a lucky person who never once found themselves at rock bottom, calling out to God for help? My grandfather – on my mother's side – and all my uncles were fishermen. And they were all God-fearing men. But they could tell you, a fisherman out in a wild sea may never darken the doors of any church, but if a towering black wave threatens to capsize his boat, he'll know how to pray all right; and anyone who has ever stood at the bedside of someone they love who is dying, will know that running behind all words are silent prayers – even if they are to a God they think they don't believe in. It isn't something you have to be taught, it comes as naturally as breathing.

One day, when I was still working at the Co-op in Morecambe, someone came in and said, "Will you come home, Thora. Your mother has been taken very ill." It was dreadful. The manager saw my face and said at once, "Yes, you run along."

I remember so vividly running to the house. I was still wearing my shop overall. When I got there the doctor was with her, putting a hot-water bottle behind her back, and doing what he could, you know, to make her more comfortable. She had had her first heart attack. Of course, if it had been today, an ambulance would have been sent for and taken her straight into hospital. She might have made a complete recovery. It wasn't like that in those days.

I can remember running upstairs to my old room, where she had sat on the bed and listened to my nightly prayers for so many years when I was little. And I knelt by the bed and prayed: "Please, please, God, don't let her die. Get her well, so we can all look after her." I don't know, really, why I felt I needed to go there. I was a married woman with a home of my own, so it wasn't even "my" room any longer. You can pray anywhere, can't you? But I suppose I thought that God might hear me better from there.

Thankfully my mother lived another eight years. We cared for her, it was very loving, and she continued to give all of us so much love. But she was dreadfully ill.

I've sometimes wondered since, who was I praying for – her or for myself? Would it have been better, for her sake, if she had quietly gone to her rest then? But then I think, we are all in God's hands, and perhaps he spared her to us for as long as possible, because there were still many things we had to learn, about giving as well as receiving love and care. So it wasn't just because I begged him.

Here are some heartfelt prayers born out of fear and trouble:

> Dear God, be good to me;
> the sea is so wide,
> and my boat is so small.
>
> Breton Fisherman

> O Western wind, when wilt thou blow
> That the small rain down shall rain?
> Christ, that my love were in my arms,
> And I in my bed again!
>
> Epitaph – Anon.

> I have gone astray like a sheep that is lost:
> O seek thy servant. Psalm 119:176 (AV)

I will lift up mine eyes unto the hills:
from whence cometh my help.

Psalm 121:1 (AV)

I love the Lord, for he heard my voice;
he heard my cry for mercy.
Because he turned his ear to me,
I will call on him as long as I live.

The cords of death entangled me,
the anguish of the grave came upon me;
I was overcome by trouble and sorrow.
Then I called on the name of the Lord:
"O Lord, save me!"   Psalm 116:1–4 (NIV)

Out of the deep have I called unto thee, O Lord:
Lord, hear my voice.   Psalm 130:1 (AV)

Then Peter got down out of the boat,
walked on the water and came towards
Jesus. But when he saw the wind, he was
afraid and, beginning to sink, cried out,
"Lord, save me!"   Matthew 14:29–30 (NIV)

. . . at Gethsemane
My Father, if it is possible, may this cup be taken
  from me.
Yet not as I will, but as you will.

Matthew 26:39 (NIV)

Joy

*

**Jesus first
Others second
Yourself last**

I don't know where I first heard that little acronym, but I've always remembered it. If you want to do more than just send up "arrow" prayers to God for help in an emergency, it's a good and golden rule to remember: Jesus first, others second, yourself last: JOY. Have you noticed how many people who live by prayer seem to almost glow with an inner joy? Just like Mother Teresa.

I was lucky. I had a mother who taught me how to say my prayers, who always sat on the edge of the bed while my brother Neville and I said our prayers kneeling by our beds, before tucking us up and kissing us "Good night. God bless." The good Lord has been receiving a nightly bulletin from Thora ever since – he knows the lot!

Mothers start teaching children to say their bedtime prayers – or they did in my day – because there is a long night ahead, and most children are afraid of the dark. Saying prayers with them before they went to sleep was as good as giving them a little night-light, and made them feel safer. (Actually, I always had a night-light as well – but that's beside the point!) When you grow older nightfall can still be a worrying time, and sometimes even the days can seem to stretch endlessly ahead of you.

The Diary has a big place in Scotty's and my life. We keep it next to the telephone, and I'm here to tell you, we'd be in an unholy muddle without it! A diary full of appointments gives you a nice feeling of business and purpose, and things to look forward to. But none of us really knows what's going to happen to us, even in the next minute.

When the unexpected suddenly happens, we realize how little all those dates in our diaries mean. If I was looking forward to something really exciting, like meeting the Queen herself, and something happened to Jan or Scotty and they needed me, the appointment with the Queen would have to come second.

Of course, I would try to get a message to Her Majesty, and write her a nice letter afterwards to apologize and explain! (Well, I can dream, can't I?!)

I'm not someone who is very fond of their own company, and it makes me sad when I hear from people who have to spend a lot of their time alone, even at Christmas and on their birthdays. Too many people have to live like that – so alone.

Praying is knowing that the Lord is with you all the time – in all your unknown future, as well as in the past. Life is beautiful, but it is also shot through with pain. And I'm not just talking about angina and arthritis, although I know all about them! We all get hurt, however full or however empty our day-to-day lives may seem. People we love die. We fall in love and have our hearts broken. We quarrel with our children. We grow lonely. We feel useless. People at work seem to be trying to do us down. But when we talk to the

Lord about these things, we find he knows all about it. He is always there, in the middle of it all, waiting to show us how to learn and grow. And then, as the hymn says: You will go out with JOY!

When the disciples asked Jesus to teach them how to pray, he told them to think of God as their loving father as well as their king – someone who really knew them and understood them and loved them.

The Lord's Prayer

Our Father, who art in heaven,
Hallowed be thy name.
Thy kingdom come,
Thy will be done,
    on earth as it is in heaven.
Give us this day our daily bread,
And forgive us our trespasses,
    as we forgive them that trespass against us,
And lead us not into temptation,
But deliver us from evil.

For thine is the kingdom, the power, and the glory
    for ever and ever.

Talking to the Lord

✳

The Royal Telephone

CHORUS:
Telephone to glory, O this joy Divine,
I can feel the current moving on the line;
Praise I give the Father for his very own,
Telephone to glory on this royal telephone!

1

Central's never busy, always on the line,
You can hear from heaven almost any time:
'Tis a royal service built for one and all,
When you get in trouble, give this
    royal line a call.

(CHORUS)

2

There will be no charges, telephone is free.
It is good for service just for you and me.
There will be no waiting on this royal line,
Telephone to glory, he answers just in time.

(CHORUS)

3

Telephone to glory, O this joy Divine,
I can feel the current moving on the line;
Praise I give the Father for his very own,
Telephone to glory on this royal telephone!

Anon
(As sung by Glasgow Youth Choir)

꽁꽁꽁 ✿ ꛷꛷꛷

Do you remember seeing Agnes Hoey conducting the
children from the Glasgow Youth Choir, singing this
song so bouncily on *Praise Be!* last year? I got so many
letters asking for the words and music afterwards!
And whenever I get a lot of letters asking me to send
the words of a particular song or prayer, I always think
there must be so many more, who would also dearly
like to have them but who somehow just never get
round to writing. So "Telephone to Glory" is for all of
them – but there is a snag: I haven't been able to find a
hymn book with the original words in.

What happened was that Agnes Hoey heard this
song being sung somewhere, and wrote the words
down as fast as she could. But there were some gaps,
which she filled in with her own words, so the version
I've given you is the Agne Hoey version, which may
not be exactly the same as the "Authorized Version", if
you'll pardon the expression. So I hope the writer of
the original song will forgive both Agnes Hoey and
me, and perhaps they'd like to write to me, so I can
discover his or her name. Any road up, I think it's a
great song, and the words fit in nicely here, because,
after all, what is "telephoning to Glory" if it isn't
praying?

When I was in *Allelujah!* the character I played,
Salvation Army Captain Emily Ridley, was a great girl
for talking to the Lord – not kneeling down to pray
formally, or during a service, but, you know, she
would chat away to him through the day, as though
heaven were just a few inches above her nose. As
that's exactly what I do myself, I didn't have any
difficulty in playing the role!

I sing hymns while I'm dusting and hoovering the house (sometimes Scotty makes it a duet!) – and that's a form of praying, too, because all hymns are sung for God. But what I enjoy most is just chatting to him, like I do to you.

Take the other day. I was going through the post and amongst it I opened two letters, one after the other, which both contained money – a ten pound note in one, and a twenty pound note in the next one – both asking me to donate it to the charity of my choice. And I thought, "Oh dear, Lord! Whichever charity shall I send it to?" Well, the very next letter I opened came from a leprosy hospital, asking for help. I've always previously thought of leprosy as "that thing they had in the Bible", but, as this letter said, millions of people are still suffering from it. The only difference is that today we know how to cure it – but it costs money. Like everything else.

So that's what I think the Lord was saying to me. I really think that. I think the Lord heard me asking, and answered, "Thora, please send the money to help cure people with leprosy." So I did.

I'm sure many prayers start off as conversations with the Lord, and then they have been written down later. A faithful *Praise Be!* viewer, Clemency Greatorex from Goudhurst, sent me this prayer, which I read out one year, and afterwards I received many requests for copies.

Clemency calls it "Martha's Prayer", but I bet it grew out of some of your own private chats with the Lord, didn't it, Clemency?

Lord, defend me from feeling hard-done by
when the chores seem endless.
Forgive me when I am bored
by the constantly recurring need to think about food.
Teach me to organize myself
in order not to be rushed
but never to be ruled by organization
and always to have time to listen.
Make me laugh, not swear,
when the milk boils over.
Preserve me from getting in a fuss
when the Grand-Joneses are coming to dinner.
Let me thank You daily for my home,
for warmth and food,
and for my friends and family.
Lord, remind me often
that it takes Martha as well as Mary
to serve You perfectly.

Clemency Greatorex 1983

And here is someone else talking to the Lord:

> O God, I am Mustafah, the Tailor,
> and I work at the shop of Muhammed Ali.
> The whole day long I sit
> and pull the needle and the thread through the cloth.
> O God, you are the needle and I am the thread.
> I am attached to you and I follow you.
> When the thread tries to slip away from the needle
> it becomes tangled up,
> and must be cut,
> so that it can be put back in the right place.
> O God, help me to follow you wherever you may
>   lead me.
> For I am really only Mustafah, the Tailor,
> and I work at the shop of Muhammed Ali –
> on the great square.
>
> > Amen

That was a Muslim's prayer – so you see, we're not so far apart as some people think.

Not everyone finds it easy to think of eloquent things to say when they pray – but it doesn't really matter – it's thinking of God as your loving friend that counts.

I remember hearing on the wireless not so long ago about a man called Jim. This Jim would be seen going into his local church every morning on his way to work, and a few seconds later he'd come straight out again, and be on his way.

The vicar, when he noticed this, couldn't resist asking Jim one day, "What do you *do* when you go into the church in the mornings, Jim? You're so quick!"

And Jim replied, "Well – I just say: 'Hallo, Jesus. It's Jim.'"

Some time later Jim fell ill and was in hospital. He had few visitors, because he had no family, but it was noticeable that he had a very good effect on everybody else in the ward. The whole atmosphere became peaceful and pleasant. One of the nurses remarked on this to Jim, who said it wasn't him, it was his visitor. The nurse said, "But Jim, you hardly get any visitors!"

"Yes I do," said Jim. "Every morning my visitor comes in and says, 'Hallo, Jim. It's Jesus.'"

> "So I say to you: Ask, and it will be given to you; seek and you will find; knock and the door will be opened to you. For everyone who asks receives; he who seeks finds; and to him who knocks, the door will be opened." Luke 11:9–10 (NIV)

Prayers for the day ahead

✳

This is the day which the Lord hath made;
we will rejoice and be glad in it.

Psalm 118

As I've already mentioned, I sometimes have to finish
my night-time petitions the following morning. And
sometimes I add one or two of these prayers and
verses, which viewers of *Praise Be!* have written out
and kindly sent to me over the years.

> Do all the good you can
> By all the means you can
> In all the ways you can
> At all the times you can
> To all the people you can
> As long as you can.

John Wesley's rule for living

I expect to pass through this world but
once; any good thing, therefore, that I can
do, or any kindness that I can show to any
fellow-creature, let me do it now; let me not
defer or neglect it, for I shall not pass this
way again.   Stephen Grellet

Teach us, good Lord, to serve thee as thou deservest;
to give and not to count the cost;
to fight and not to heed the wounds;
to toil, and not to seek for rest;
to labour, and to ask for no reward,
save that of knowing that we do thy will.

St Ignatius Loyola (1491–1556)

O Lord God, when thou givest to thy
servants to endeavour any great matter,
grant us also to know that it is not the
beginning, but the continuing of the same
unto the end, until it be thoroughly
finished, which yieldeth the true glory;
through him who for the finishing of thy
work laid down his life, our Redeemer,
Jesus Christ.   After Sir Francis Drake

The things, good Lord, that we pray for,
give us the grace to labour for.

St Thomas More, 1478–1535

Christ be with me, Christ within me,
Christ behind me, Christ before me,
Christ beside me, Christ to win me,
Christ to comfort and restore me.
Christ beneath me, Christ above me,
Christ in quiet, Christ in danger,
Christ in hearts of all who love me,
Christ in mouth of friend or stranger.

St Patrick's Breastplate

The day returns and brings us the petty round of irritating concerns and duties . . '. Help us to perform them with laughter and kind faces, let cheerfulness abound with industry. Give us to go blithely on our business all this day, bring us to our resting beds weary and content and un-dishonoured, and grant us in the end the gift of sleep.

Robert Louis Stevenson (1850–94)

From tomorrow on I shall be sad.
From tomorrow on.
Not today. Today I will be glad.
And every day, no matter how bitter it may be,
I shall say:
From tomorrow on I shall be sad,
not today.   From a child in a Nazi Death Camp
(in *Short Prayers for the Long Day*)

Lord, for tomorrow and its needs,
I do not pray;
But keep me, guide me, love me, Lord,
Just for today.   Anon
Just for Today

So do not worry, saying "What shall we eat?" or "What shall we drink?" or "What shall we wear?" For the pagans run after all these things, and your heavenly Father knows that you need them. But seek first his kingdom and his righteousness, and all these things will be given to you as well. Therefore do not worry about tomorrow, for tomorrow will worry about itself. Each day has enough trouble of its own.

Matthew 6:31–34 (NIV)

Seasonal Prayers

✳

I had a full week, the week before last Christmas. I went to Nottingham, and announced the carols at a Methodist church there, for their Carolcade. Well, I knew at once it was a loved and cherished place, from the strong smell of Mansion polish – but I suppose I might have thought more about it probably also being nearly lethal! The pulpit steps were wooden, and lovely and shiny, so I reached out to hold the big, highly polished, round knob at the top of the hand-rail, and I had nearly reached the top, when I suddenly disappeared from view! I was all right, though, and we had a lovely service.

Then, back in London, I went for morning coffee and mince pies at the Methodist church at West-minster Central Hall, which was beautiful. The Minister, the Rev. Dr John Tudor – a dear friend – does this every Christmas, to thank everybody for helping during the year.

And then I went on to join the congregation for their lunchtime Carolcade in Wesley's Chapel in the City Road. It's known as "The Cathedral of World Methodism" and was where John Wesley spent the last twelve years of his life, and where he is buried. Visitors come from all over the world, to look over John Wesley's house, and visit the Chapel, which he had built, with the Museum of Methodism in the crypt. They have even still got one tier of the actual pulpit he preached from, so it's like a place of pilgrimage for Methodists.

It was *packed* – all with people from the City, coming in their lunch hour. There was a cracking sermon by Dr Colin Morris, and what was rather nice, the Japanese chairman of Nissan UK read one of the lessons. I don't know if he was a Methodist. I was in a bit of pain, and had to be helped to the lectern, and I said to them, "I don't usually have to be helped, but the other day – I Fell on My Way to The Pulpit!" It sounds like the first line of a Victorian Monologue, doesn't it?

The carol I chose there was "While Shepherds Watched their Flocks by Night", to the tune "Lyngham" – the one you probably associate with "O For a Thousand Tongues to Sing". And I told them the reason – because for me, that's the *right* tune. It's the one I always remember the Sally Army Band playing, every Christmas, when they'd come down Cheapside and play and sing carols early on Christmas morning.

So we all sang it, and they had even got a Salvation Army Band up in the gallery, to play it. And I told them: "That's the best Christmas present I'll have this year."

> While shepherds wa-a-a-a-atched
> Their flo-ocks by-y night
> All seated on the ground
> All sea-ea-ea-ea-eated on the ground,
> The angel o-o-of the Lo-o-ord came down
> And glory shone around
> And glory shone around
> And glo-o-o-ory shone around!

There are carols and hymns for every season of the year, and I like to try and include them all on *Praise Be!* When it come to prayers, there's a special one for every single Sunday. Many members of the Church of England – especially the older ones – know by heart all of the Sunday Collects from the Book of Common Prayer, through hearing them repeated year by year. Younger Christians will be more used to the ones in their new books, but they don't seem quite so special somehow. Well, I don't think so. The old collects are beautiful, short prayers written – oh, centuries ago – by Thomas Cranmer, one for each Sunday of the year. In my *Praise Be! Christmas Book* I mentioned one of my favourites:

> Stir up, we beseech thee, O Lord, the wills of thy faithful people; that they, plenteously bringing forth the fruit of good works, may of thee be plenteously rewarded.

Well, you see, it's always said at the end of November, and the words are a very useful reminder that it's time to "stir up" and "bring forth the fruit of good works" – i.e. make the Christmas pudding!

You can find all the collects in the Prayer Book, but here is a selection of them – for those of you who, like me, weren't brought up in the Church of England. We Methodists are more used to hearing inspired prayers spoken by the Minister, more or less "ad lib" you might say. But it's nice to have a good script sometimes, and that Archbishop Cranmer certainly knew how to write a good 'un! You may be surprised to find how familiar the words of many of them are.

First Sunday in Advent (December)

Almighty God, give us grace that we may cast away the works of darkness, and put upon us the armour of light, now in the time of this mortal life, in which thy Son Jesus Christ came to visit us in great humility; that in the last day, when he shall come again in his glorious Majesty, to judge both the quick and the dead, we may rise to the life immortal.

Second Sunday in Advent

Blessed Lord, who hast caused all holy Scriptures to be written for our learning:

Grant that we may in such wise hear them, read, mark, learn, and inwardly digest them, that by patience and comfort of thy holy Word, we may embrace and ever hold fast the blessed hope of everlasting life, which thou hast given us in our Saviour Jesus Christ.

Fouth Sunday after Epiphany

O God, who knowest us to be set in the midst of so many and great dangers, that by reason of the frailty of our nature we cannot always stand upright:

Grant to us such strength and protection, as may support us in all dangers, and carry us through all temptations.

Quinquagesima (Sunday before Lent)

O Lord, who hast taught us that all our doings without charity are nothing worth:

Send thy Holy Ghost, and pour into our hearts that most excellent gift of charity, the very bond of peace and of all virtues, without which whosoever liveth is counted dead before thee.

Ash Wednesday (First day of Lent)

Almighty and everlasting God, who hatest nothing that thou hast made, and dost forgive the sins of all them that are penitent:

Create and make in us new and contrite hearts, that we, worthily lamenting our sins, and acknowledging our wretchedness, may obtain of thee, the God of all mercy, perfect remission and forgiveness.

Second Sunday in Lent

Almighty God, who seest that we have no power of ourselves to help ourselves:

Keep us both outwardly in our bodies, and inwardly in our souls; that we may be defended from all adversities which may happen to the body, and from all evil thoughts which may assault and hurt the soul.

Fourth Sunday after Easter

O Almighty God, who alone canst order the unruly wills and affections of sinful men:

Grant unto thy people, that they may love the thing which thou commandest, and desire that which thou dost promise; that so, among the sundry and manifold changes of the world, our hearts may surely there be fixed, where true joys are to be found.

Fourth Sunday after Trinity

O God, the protector of all that trust in thee, without whom nothing is strong, nothing is holy:

Increase and multiply upon us thy mercy; that, thou being our ruler and guide, we may so pass through things temporal, that we finally lose not the things eternal.

Twenty-first Sunday after Trinity

Grant, we beseech thee, merciful Lord, to thy faithful people pardon and peace; that they may be cleansed from all their sins, and serve thee with a quiet mind; through Jesus Christ our Lord, Amen.

Grace

*

Give us, Lord, a bit o' sun,
A bit o' work and a bit o' fun;
Give us all in the struggle and sputter
Our daily bread and a bit o' butter.

On the wall of an inn in Lancashire

I wonder how many people still say grace before their meals. I expect some *Praise Be!* viewers do. Scotty and I don't really, except when it's a special feast, at Christmas and Thanksgiving and Easter. We'll be in the country, at Jan's, with all the family, and Jan usually says grace, and I always think, "How nice." But as I'm always thanking the Lord every day for so many different things, I don't make a special point of thanking him for my lunch. I thank Scotty for that most days! But I know that some people wouldn't feel right about sitting down at table without saying grace, even when they are on their own.

There are some beautiful graces you can say, and I've heard and shared in hundreds of them at charity "dos" I go to. Sometimes we even sing the doxology as a grace:

Praise God, from whom all blessings flow
Praise Him, all creatures here below
Praise Him above, ye heavenly host
Praise Father, Son and Holy Ghost.

Here is a little collection of graces I've come across –
some of them really make you think.

Be present at our table, Lord,
Be here and everywhere adored.
Thy creatures bless, and grant that we
May feast in paradise with Thee.

John Wesley

In a somewhere hungry,
sometimes lonely world,
for food and friends
we give you thanks, O Lord.

A Unitarian grace

Benedictus Benedicat

(a Roman Catholic Latin grace – must be the
shortest on record! It takes longer to say in
English, and means "May He who is blessed
give his blessing.")

Some hae meat and canna eat,
And some would eat that want it;
But we hae meat, and we can eat,
And sae the Lord be thankit.

Robert Burns
The Selkirk Grace

All good gifts around us
Are sent from heaven above;
Then thank the Lord, O thank the Lord,
For all his love.   M. Claudius, Tr. Jane Campbell

Here a little child I stand
Heaving up my either hand;
Cold as paddocks though they be,
Here I lift them up to Thee,
For a benison to fall
On our meat and on us all.

Robert Herrick

Blessed art Thou
O Lord our God
King of the Universe
Who bringest forth bread from the earth.

From the Hebrew Prayer Book.
They say this every Sunday morning on "This is
the Day", the BBC 1 television service

Bless this Mess!
From the Bishops' Cookbook
sold in aid of the Church Urban Fund.

While they were eating, Jesus took bread, gave
thanks and broke it.   Matthew 26:26 (NIV)

Pilgrim Prayers

*

Every time I see a church
I always go and visit
So when at last I'm carried in
The Lord won't say:
"Who is it?"

Note found pinned in porch of Old Romney church
while filming *Praise Be!* 1987

Oh dear! was it really that long ago that *Praise Be!* and I
visited those beautiful churches on Romney Marsh?
Five years!

Scotty doesn't really enjoy driving any more, but we
often used to go for little outings in the car, and many's
the time we've stopped in some pretty little village for
a cuppa in an olde worlde tea shoppe, and there will
often be a lovely old parish church nearby to visit. I
always think it's surprising how huge some of them
are, when the village itself might consist of just a few
little cottages. When our ancestors built houses for
God they built 'em big! I always remember one of my
great-uncles, who worked on Liverpool Anglican
Cathedral all his working life, and when he died, it still
wasn't finished!

I've collected for this chapter prayers for pilgrims.
Just because you arrive in a car or a coach, doesn't
mean you are not a pilgrim!

Among the daily crowds of visitors to the great
cathedrals like Canterbury or Chester or York or St

David's or Winchester, many really are pilgrims, who want to add their prayers to those of the hundreds and thousands of Christians who have made their way there over the centuries. And as well as the cathedrals, there are all those holy places – like Glastonbury, Iona and Lindisfarne. Some people go further still, to Assisi, where St Francis was born; to Lourdes and Medjugorje, scenes of visions and healing miracles; to Rome, where there are so many beautiful churches and relics of the earliest days of Christianity; to Taizé, in Northern France, a community founded to be a centre for reconciliation after the Second World War. Today thousands of young people make their way there, from all over the world. Scotty and I have been among the millions of pilgrims who have been to Jerusalem and visited the Holy Land.

Each year for *Praise Be!* I make little pilgrimages, too. Sometimes I've been looking for places where our much loved hymns were written or inspired, like the rock at Burrington Combe in the Mendips, where the Rev. Augustus Toplady was said to have sheltered from a storm in a cleft, which inspired the words of "Rock of Ages"; and Horbury Bridge, where Sabine Baring-Gould wrote my favourite: "Onward Christian Soldiers" for his Sunday School children to sing in a Whitsunday procession.

We've also visited some of the traditional places of pilgrimage, including the most famous of all, the seat of Archbishops and saints – Augustine, Dunstan, Anselm, Thomas – Canterbury Cathedral. I had a wonderful guide in Canon Derek Ingram-Hill, who knew every nook and cranny.

I was especially moved to find myself standing in the space they call The Martyrdom, where St Thomas

Becket was murdered when he was Archbishop; the same spot where, in May 1982, Archbishop Robert Runcie and Pope John Paul II knelt side by side and prayed for reconciliation. We all watched on television – an unforgettable image, and probably the only occasion when "Two People Praying" has been the lead item on the national and international television news!

> May the road rise to meet you.
> May the wind be always at your back.
> May the sun shine warm upon your face,
> the rains fall soft upon your fields,
> and until we meet again,
> may God hold you in the palm of his hand.

An Irish Blessing

Canterbury

Heavenly Father, you have brought us to the place
where the Christian faith was rooted again;
to the shrine of martyrs and prophets;
to the throne of Archbishops;
to the home of scholars and saints;
and to the Mother Church of our
    Anglican Communion.
Lead us by your Spirit, in our pilgrimage to
    Canterbury,
and by that Spirit, kindle in our hearts
gratitude for the past,
and hope for the years ahead,
through Jesus Christ our Lord.

> Prayer of the Birmingham Diocesan Pilgrimage
> to Canterbury 1986

Chichester

Thanks be to thee, my Lord Jesus Christ,
For all the benefits which thou hast given to me,
For all the pains and insults which thou has borne
    for me.
O most merciful redeemer, friend and brother,
May I know thee more clearly,
Love thee more dearly,
And follow thee more nearly,
Day by day.

> Prayer of St Richard of Chichester d. 1253

Chester

Heavenly Father,
as we follow in the footsteps of our forefathers
on our pilgrimage of faith,
fill us with your heavenly grace
and so make us faithful witnesses to all people
of the love of Jesus.
Grant that we, being firmly grounded
in the truth of the Gospel,
may be faithful to its teaching,
both in word and deed,
through Christ our Lord.

Prayer for pilgrims used by the Cathedral

Norwich

Jesus . . . answered: "It behoved that there
should be sin; but all shall be well, and all
shall be well, and all manner of things shall
be well . . ."
"Thou shalt not be overcome," was said full
     clearly . . .
He said not, "Thou shalt not be tempested,
thou shalt not be travailed,
thou shalt not be dis-eased," but he said
"Thou shalt not be overcome."

Julian of Norwich (14th century)
from "Revelations of Divine Love"

York

Grant us, Lord,
in thought, faith;
in word, wisdom;
in deed, courage;
in life, service;
through Jesus Christ our Lord.

> Prayer at the nave altar

Iona

Almighty and everlasting, God of our fathers,
Guide unto our children's children,
we the frail creatures of a passing day
come once more in thy presence
to renew our vows unto thee
and to ask thee, unworthy though we be,
to renew for us thy presence.

> Prayer of Rev. George MacLeod –
> founder of Iona Community

Bless to me, O God, the earth beneath my feet,
Bless to me, O God, the path whereon I go,
Bless to me, O God, the people whom I meet,
Today, tonight and tomorrow. Amen.

Ancient Celtic prayer used by the Iona Community at
the start of each weekly pilgrimage around the island

Taizé

Christ, Saviour of every life, you come to us always.
Welcoming you in the peace of our nights,
in the silence of our days,
in the beauty of creation,
in the hours of intense combat,
welcoming you means knowing
that you will be with us in every situation, always.

Prayer of Brother Roger of Taizé

I sometimes like to make a *very* short pilgrimage –
down to our own little church! It's a pleasant walk
down a long country lane (lovingly kept tidy and in
good order by one of the parishioners, because there's
a lot of "following" with a lane – which means it takes a
lot of looking after, in case you didn't know!). At the
back of our Church Guide there's a prayer for all us
pilgrims:

May your pilgrimage here give you fresh
  inspiration for life's pilgrimage.
May you have an increased sense of
  wonder at the natural beauty of this part
  of Sussex, in which this village church is
  so superbly set.
May you have an increased sense of
  appreciation of the artistic skill, and
  religious faith, of our forefathers.
May you have an increased sense of
  gratitude to God for all his many gifts.
And may you have a safe journey home.

The Holy Land

May the babe of Bethlehem be yours to tend;
May the boy of Nazareth be yours to friend;
May the man of Galilee his healing send;
May the Christ of Calvary his courage lend;
May the risen Lord his presence send;
And his holy angels defend you, to the end.

Canon Ronald Brownrigg b. 1919,
based on words of Father George Potter of Peckham

Anyone who has sat with their fellow pilgrims in a little boat in the middle of the Sea of Galilee, and joined in with the singing of this next hymn, will have had an unforgettable experience of pilgrimage and prayer. The old hills all round the lake still stand, looking just the same as they would have done to Jesus and his disciples.

Dear Lord and Father of mankind,
Forgive our foolish ways!
Reclothe us in our rightful mind,
In purer lives Thy service find,
In deeper reverence praise.

In simple trust like theirs who heard,
Beside the Syrian sea,
The gracious calling of the Lord,
Let us, like them, without a word
Rise up and follow Thee.

O Sabbath rest by Galilee!
O calm of hills above,
Where Jesus knelt to share with Thee
The silence of eternity,
Interpreted by love!

Drop Thy still dews of quietness,
Till all our strivings cease;
Take from our souls the strain and stress,
And let our ordered lives confess
The beauty of Thy peace.

Breathe through the hearts of our desire
Thy coolness and Thy balm;
Let sense be dumb, let flesh retire,
Speak through the earthquake, wind and fire,
O still small voice of calm!

John Greenleaf Whittier (1802–92)

After this the Lord appointed seventy-two
others, and sent them two by two ahead of
him to every town and place where he was
about to go. He told them, "The harvest is
plentiful, but the workers are few. Ask the
Lord of the harvest, therefore, to send out
workers into his harvest field. Go! I am
sending you out like lambs among wolves."

Luke 10:1–3 (NIV)

Before the "Big Night"

*

Put your trust in God, my boys, and keep
your powder dry.   Valentine Blacker

For years I always said a little prayer as I was standing
in the wings of a theatre, waiting for my first entrance:
"Please God, help me to give them a good perform-
ance tonight."

Then in 1974, my brother Neville got cancer. So I
always added "and please comfort Neville, and make
him better."

I was in "No, No Nanette" at Drury Lane at the time,
and something suddenly seemed to dawn on me,
because the two parts of the prayer just didn't seem
comparable. I thought, "Why have I been saying this
prayer every night? The Lord has given me my talent –
I must just get on with it. My heartfelt prayers should
be for Neville, and for things I *can't* do anything
about." So I said:

"Please help Neville now. I'm sorry I've been asking
you to help me for so many years. I'll do the best I can
with what you've given me."

All the same, it's nice to be reminded and reassured
of God's presence when you are about to do something difficult or frightening.

Lord, help me to remember
that nothing is going to happen today
that you and I together
can't handle!   Anon

"Let's look for dragons," I said to Pooh.
"Yes, let's," said Pooh to me.
We crossed the river and found a few –
"Yes, those are dragons all right," said Pooh,
"As soon as I saw their beaks I knew
That's what they are," said Pooh, said he.
"That's what they are," said Pooh.

"Let's frighten the dragons," I said to Pooh.
"That's right," said Pooh to me.
"I'm not afraid," I said to Pooh,
And I held his paw and I shouted "Shoo!
Silly old dragons!" – and off they flew.
"I wasn't afraid," said Pooh, said he,
"I'm never afraid with you."

A. A. Milne (1882–1956) from "Us Two"

God, give us grace to accept with serenity
the things we cannot change, courage to
change the things we must, and the
wisdom to know the difference.

Reinhold Niebuhr 1892–1971

O Lord, thou knowest how busy I must be this day; if I forget thee, do not thou forget me: for Christ's sake.

General Lord Astley (1579–1652)
before the battle of Edgehill

I bind unto myself today
the power of God to hold and lead;
his eye to watch, his might to stay,
his ear to hearken to my need;
the wisdom of my God to teach,
his hand to guide, his shield to ward,
the word of God to give me speech,
his heavenly host to be my guard.

St Patrick's Breastplate

Then Jesus looked up towards heaven and prayed, "Father, the time has come. Glorify your Son, that your Son may glorify you."

John 17:1 (NIV)

All Things Bright and Beautiful

✳

Let all things their Creator bless,
And worship him in humbleness;
O praise him, alleluia!

W. H. Draper
based on St Francis' Canticle of the Sun

We never forget the love and fun that animals bring into our lives on *Praise Be!* I get lots of letters telling me about the important place these "friends" have in your hearts.

One year we visited the Donkey Sanctuary in Sidmouth, where I met Elizabeth Svendsen and she did me the great honour of naming a new-born donkey after me: Thor! He's still doing very well, they tell me – a little grey donkey, like a small thundercloud, bless him!

Oh! I've met all creatures great and small on my travels with *Praise Be!* One year we went to Les and Sue Stocker's Wildlife Hospital, St Tiggywinkles, when it was still based in their own backyard, with their dining room as head office! They've got more land, and a much bigger place now, a proper teaching hospital, and Les got the MBE in the 1991 New Year Honours List, for all the work they do rescuing and healing wild animals that have been injured – usually by people with cars, shotguns or traps. I remember when I was there holding a tiny hedgehog in my hand,

and he peered up at me and blinked, the dear little thing.

Jan's greatly beloved dogs and ducks always have a big part to play in the programmes, following me all round the garden. Patch and Tess, the two dogs – there were three, but our dear little Lucy died a few years ago – always come and listen when I read "The Dog's Prayer" on *Praise Be!*

——————

O Lord of all creatures, grant that man, my master, may be as faithful to other men as I am to him.

Make him as loving towards his family and friends as I am loving to him.

Grant that he may guard with honesty the good things with which Thou hast endowed him, as honestly as I guard him.

Give him, O Lord, a happy and ready smile, as happy and spontaneous as the wagging of my tail. Make him as ready to show gratitude as I am eager to lick his hand.

Give him patience as great as mine when I await his return.

Grant him my courage and my readiness to sacrifice all for him, even my own life.

May he possess my youthful spirit and joy.

O Lord of all creatures, as I am in truth only a dog, may my master always be truly a man.

Anon

——————

One of my favourite discoveries for *Praise Be!* recently has been "Tailwags", a little book of "Thoughts and Prayers of an Elderly Sister", by Sister Maud CAH. Nearly all her thoughts and prayers were inspired by the natural world, in which she took such great pleasure.

If you want the little book, you can write to Sister Winifred Edith at the All Hallows Community, Ditchingham, Norfolk. But here are just one or two which I especially like. Sister Maud herself has since died – and she, like all other members of the Community, is lovingly remembered in daily prayer by the Sisters.

The nuns live in a convent set in the heart of beautiful Norfolk countryside. If you have ever visited them there, I'm sure these verses will remind you of how, wherever you happen to be – in the sitting room, dining room, or helping with the washing up in the kitchen – there always seems to be a cat nearby, gazing at you soulfully from some sunny windowsill!

Oh, and how Sister Maud used the tail-end of her life! She wrote all the thoughts and prayers collected in the book between her 80th and 90th birthdays!

Joey Protests

(on being turned out of Chapel)

Why did they turn me out?
I whispered – I didn't shout.
I WANTED to be there
With a little feline prayer.
But although I didn't shout,
They turned me out.

I don't believe they knew,
That a hushed up mew
Is the best a cat can do.
So – although it wasn't a shout,
They turned me out.

And the end of my prayer was said
Outside – on the mat – instead.

Carol for the Community of All Hallows

O we would go a-carolling,
But we are not enough;
We've many rather old ones
Whose tone is slightly rough.

(The Cats join in)

O what can we do?
They are too few!
Let us add to their song
Our soft little "mew"
"Mew . . . Mew . . . Mew . . ."

And though the Babe rejoices
At the soft "Mew" sounds
The song still scarcely voices
The joy that abounds.

(The Poultry join in)

O what can we do?
They are still too few:
Let us join to their song
Our "Cock-a-doodle-do"
"Cock-a-doodle-do"!

And now the song is swelling
As we all take part,
But it seems to lack foundation
To complete its art.

(The Bees join in)

O what can we do
To help these few?
Let the whole hive come
With its deep bass hum –
"Hummm . . . Hummm . . . Hummm-m.

And so we bring our offering
One and all!
And I think the Babe is smiling
In the Cattle-stall!

On hearing a donkey bray

Today
I heard a little donkey bray;
I said, "That is a ghastly sound!"
But looking round
I saw an angel standing near
Stroking its ear.
"Maybe," he said, "that is his way
To pray –
And maybe he is thanking God
For that lush green sod . . .
And could it be that when you think you're praying
God sometimes hears a faint discordant braying?"

Ye shall find an ass tied, and a colt with her:
loose them, and bring them unto me.
   And if any man say ought unto you, ye
shall say, "The Lord hath need of them."

Matthew 21·2–3 (AV)

Getting On

*

"Only the tail-end of life is left," I said;
And into my head
A thought came out of the blue,
A thought from You –
"But that is the cheery end," You said
"So see
That you use it for Me."
And I said, "Amen," and raised my head.
"I will glorify God with a wag," I said.

Tailwag No. 1
Sister Maud CAH

I recently visited the Royal Star and Garter Home for disabled sailors, soldiers and airmen. I had been invited to present a new hymn book that they'd had prepared, one with very large print, because some of the old boys there had been saying, "I can't read my hymn book. The print's too small."

I am a fortunate woman to be invited to such an occasion. And I said to them all at the end: "There is one thing I don't want you to do, and that is to thank me for coming. It's been just such a joy and a pleasure. Tell me, do you have Carolthon or anything like that here at Christmas time?"

They said, "Oh, yes, we have a beautiful carol concert." So I said, "Right! Well I'm inviting myself now, for next year!"

Because, you know, I was thinking – whatever little thing I did for them, it could never compare with what they have done for us.

Nursing the Elderly

He was a child before we were born –
Now he is helpless, old and forlorn.
He was a husband long years ago,
He walked with his wife, their cheeks all aglow.
His wife was a mother; she had babes at her breast,
Caring for others, and giving her best.
He was a man, salute him for this,
Now he is withered, and harder to kiss.
Speak to him gently, and nurse him with pride,
Now, as he waits to sail with the tide.
Ours are the last hands he'll ever hold.
Let him know love, now he is old.

Kathy Doyle
(Written while nursing the Pensioners
at the Royal Hospital, Chelsea)

Grow old along with me!
The best is yet to be,
The last of life, for which the first was made:
Our times are in His hand
Who saith, "A whole I planned,
Youth shows but half; trust God: see all, nor be afraid!"

Robert Browning
from "Rabbi Ben Ezra"

I'll never forget the sackfuls of letters I received, all asking me to send you the words, when I read the following prayer on *Prayer Be!* one year.

The Nun's Prayer

Lord, Thou knowest better than I know myself that I am growing older and will some day be old. Keep me from the fatal habit of thinking I must say something on every subject, and on every occasion. Release me from craving to straighten out everybody's affairs.

Make me thoughtful, but not moody, helpful, but not bossy. With my vast stores of wisdom, it seems a pity not to use it all. But Thou knowest, Lord, I want a few friends at the end.

Keep me reasonably sweet. I do not want to be a saint – some of them are so hard to live with. But a sour old person is one of the crowning works of the Devil.

Keep my mind free from the recital of endless details; give me wings to get to the point.

Seal my lips on my aches and pains. They are increasing and love of rehearsing them is becoming sweeter as the years go by.

I dare not ask for grace enough to enjoy the tales of others' pains, but help me to endure them with patience.

I dare not ask for improved memory,
but for a growing humility,
and a lessening cocksureness when my memory seems to clash with the memories of others.

Teach me the glorious lesson that occasionally I may be mistaken.

Give me the ability to see good things in unexpected places, and talents in unexpected people.

And give me, O Lord, the grace to tell them so.

17th Century? Found in Rochester Cathedral

When as a child I laughed and wept –
> Time crept.
When as a youth I waxed more bold –
> Time strolled.
When I became a full grown man –
> Time ran.
When older still I grew –
> Time flew.
Soon I shall find in passing on –
> Time gone.
O Christ will Thou have saved me then –
> Amen.

> Words on the clock in Chester Cathedral

O Lord, you have made us very small, and we bring our years to an end, like a tale that is told; help us to remember that beyond our brief day is the eternity of your love.

> Reinhold Niebuhr (1982–1971)

Look at the birds of the air. They do not sow or reap or store away in barns, and yet your heavenly Father feeds them. Are you not much more valuable than they?

Who of you by worrying can add a single hour to his life?   Matthew 6:26–27 (NIV)

Coming Clean

*

It's not my brother, or my sister, but it's me, O Lord
Standing in the need of prayer.

Well, nobody's perfect! Children are always getting
themselves into scrapes while they are growing up,
and I'll be the first to admit I was in disgrace with my
parents on more than one occasion – usually for doing
something like getting carried away with enthusiasm,
and entering talent contests behind their backs! They
both loved me dearly, but I can still remember the
times I sat nervously watching my father, who would
be slowly and deliberately washing and drying his
hands on a towel when he came in from work, not
speaking, but I could almost see his brain forming the
lecture he was about to deliver. And my wonderful
mother often had to explain and put me right about
things. And, you know, she always did it in such a
gentle way that I've remembered the things she taught
me all my life.

Somehow or other, though, even if you aren't a bad
person, there are always times when you wish you
could have done things differently. We all get out of
bed the wrong side some mornings, and are snappy
with our nearest and dearest, or forgetful, or short
with a friend who has called round in need of a
patient, listening ear. It didn't mean you were a deep-
dyed villain as a child if you sometimes drove your

Dad into a rage, and it doesn't mean you're a deep-dyed villain if you sometime grieve the Lord now you're old enough to know better. You don't need to beat your breast the whole time, but it's good to turn to the Lord and own up when you know you haven't been on quite your best behaviour.

Here's what the Church of England prayer book calls the "General Confession" – for everyone to say together. And as you'll see, it covers a multitude of sins.

Almighty and most merciful Father,
we have erred and strayed from thy ways like lost
  sheep;
we have followed too much the devices and desires
  of our own hearts;
we have offended against thy holy laws;
we have left undone those things which we ought to
  have done, and we have done those things which
  we ought not to have done, and there is no health
  in us:
but thou, O Lord, have mercy upon us miserable
  offenders;
spare thou them, O God, which confess their faults;
restore thou them that are penitent, according to thy
  promises declared unto mankind in Christ Jesu
  our Lord:
and grant, O most merciful Father, for his sake, that
  we may hereafter live a godly, righteous, and
  sober life, to the glory of thy holy name.

                                                    Amen.

The sacrifice of God is a troubled spirit: a broken and contrite heart, O God, shalt thou not despise.   Psalm 51:17

"I will arise and go to my father, and will say unto him, Father, I have sinned against heaven and before thee, and am no more worthy to be called thy son."

Luke 15:18–19 (NIV)

Be ye therefore merciful, as your Father also is merciful.

Judge not, and ye shall not be judged: condemn not, and ye shall not be condemned; forgive, and ye shall be forgiven.

Luke 6:36–37 (AV)

The Son of man is come to seek and to save that which was lost.   Luke 19:10 (NIV)

Praying Together

*

And I said to the man who stood at the gate of the year: "Give me a light that I may tread safely into the unknown."

And he replied:

"Go out into the darkness, and put your hand into the hand of God. That shall be to you better than light, and safer than a known way."

from "God Knows" by Minnie Louise Haskins
(Prayer spoken by King George VI
in his 1939 Christmas message)

How many of you remember the Big Ben Minute, I wonder?

On Armistice Sunday, 10 November 1940, the BBC introduced the sound of Big Ben's chimes before the Nine O'Clock News on the wireless each night. It became known as "The Big Ben Minute for Reflection" and it was actually listed, like a real programme, in all the national newspapers and the *Radio Times*. On the previous day, Mr Howard Marshall explained the meaning of the introduction of the booming voice of Big Ben:

"Every night it will be a minute specially set apart for us to use as we will . . . some will use it for prayer, others might use it to recall the memory of the dead who were dear to them . . .

"I feel very strongly that throughout the country people are seeking a unity of purpose which goes even deeper than the deep and obvious loyalties to our common cause. We are united as a nation as we've never been before: that's quite certain. We are determined that Nazi Germany shall not be allowed to trample on everything we hold dear as free people.

"But there's something beyond that, even. We are determined that out of this world chaos shall come a better world, a world in which words like Freedom and Justice shall have a fuller meaning, and we seek a new and a finer way of life . . .

"There's no doubt that we must face the future courageously, that we must build for the future wherever we may; above all, that we must find fresh standards on which to build, and some will be seeking those standards as Big Ben strikes."

Isn't that interesting? I must confess I was always working in the theatre at nine o'clock in the evenings, so I wasn't one of the over eight million people who they reckon were joining in. But wasn't it a great idea? Because naturally everybody turned on the wireless for the Nine O'Clock News – especially during the war – and simultaneously millions could use that minute of Big Ben striking to pray for a better world. And it was extraordinary, in the war, how even during the darkest hours, when Britain was the only country left fighting Hitler, none of us seemed to doubt even for a moment that we would win. There was such a wonderful spirit, and things like the Big Ben Minute were part of it.

After the First World War the whole country used to pray together every Armistice Day, for the two minutes before the eleventh hour of the eleventh day of the eleventh month. London was like a painting for two whole minutes. Nobody and nothing moved. It felt like a year to us, standing lined up like statues in school!

And just last year, in 1991, didn't you feel it was as though it was all our prayers that were answered, when Terry Waite and all the other hostages were released from their hell-holes?

I don't suppose there are many families left nowadays who still meet for family prayers, are there? But in a funny way radio and television almost seem to provide the modern equivalent. *Praise Be!* has brought me into the homes of millions of viewers, and their letters really make me feel like part of the family. And there are many other programmes where we get the chance to exchange views and pray together across the airwaves.

For instance, if you've ever spent any time in hospital, you will have discovered you can tune in to a wonderful Hospital Radio, and they have services and times of prayer as well as playing record requests. You can ask for you favourite hymn, too, just like on *Praise Be!*

And there's – what else? the Daily Service on Radio 4, of course; and on Sundays ITV always relays a service from a different church, while BBC 1 have their "This is the Day", which is a "live" link between all the viewers who want to pray together, usually coming from one of the viewer's own homes.

During Lent in 1986 thousands of Christians from all denominations were brought together by the British Council of Churches (as it then was) from all over Northern Ireland, Scotland, England and Wales, using the local radio stations, from Shetland to Southampton, for phone-in programmes in which they tried between them to answer the question: "What on earth is the Church for?"

This is the prayer that they all prayed together each week:

Lord God, we thank you
For calling us into the company
Of those who trust in Christ
And seek to obey his will.
May your spirit guide and strengthen us
In mission and service to your world;
For we are strangers no longer
But pilgrims together
On the way to your kingdom.

Amen

You are the light of the world. A city on a hill cannot be hidden. Neither do people light a lamp and put it under a bowl. Instead they put it on its stand, and it gives light to everyone in the house. In the same way, let your light shine before men, that they may see your good deeds and praise your Father in heaven.

Matthew 5:14–16

Praying for Peace

*

Let there be peace on earth
And let it begin with me.

Whenever "Songs of Praise" comes from Northern Ireland, and you see the Protestant and Roman Catholic children – so many of them with their bright red hair and freckles, bless them! and all of them singing hymns so cheerfully together – it's almost impossible to believe that they are growing up surrounded by people who are trying to kill each other in the name of religion. God, whenever will it all end? I must confess that when they sing that hymn "Let there be peace on earth, and let it begin with me" it makes me want to cry sometimes.

When we are watching them together on *Praise Be!* I'm sure we are all quietly praying for peace to return to Northern Ireland.

Peace
be
in thy home
and
in thy heart,
or
if thou roam
Earth's
highways wide,
the Lord
be
at thy side
to bless
and guide.

© published on a prayer card by Tim Tiley Ltd.

O God of many names
Lover of all nations
We pray for peace
  in our hearts
  in our homes
  in our nations
  in our world
The peace of your will
The peace of our need.

George Appleton
(in *Oxford Book of Prayer*)

Lead me from death
to Life,
from falsehood to Truth

Lead me from despair
to Hope,
from fear to Trust

Lead me from hate
to Love,
from war to Peace

Let Peace fill our heart,
our world, our universe.

Satish Kumar
(adopted by the Prayer for Peace movement, 1981)

Lord, make me an instrument of your peace.
Where there is hatred, let me sow love,
Where there is injury, pardon;
Where there is doubt, faith;
Where there is despair, hope;
Where there is darkness, light;
Where there is sadness, joy.
O divine Master, grant that I may not so much seek
To be consoled, as to console,
To be understood, as to understand,
To be loved, as to love,
For it is in giving that we receive;
It is in pardoning that we are pardoned;
It is in dying that we are born to eternal life.

after St Francis of Assisi

Any man's death diminishes me, because I am involved in Mankind; and therefore, never send to know for whom the bell tolls: it tolls for thee.   John Donne

Blessed are the peacemakers, for they will be called sons of God.   Matthew 5:9 (NIV)

Poets' Corner

*

Let us with a gladsome mind
Praise the Lord, for he is kind,
For his mercies aye endure,
Ever faithful, ever sure.

Let us blaze His Name abroad,
For of gods he is the God;
For his mercies aye endure,
Ever faithful, ever sure.

John Milton

Some prayers are written in poetry, and many of our hymns are really sung prayers, some of them written by our greatest poets. A hymn that always seems to be more like praying than singing is Henry Lyte's beautiful "Abide with me", which every year is in the Top Ten of *Praise Be!* requests.

Abide with me; fast falls the eventide;
The darkness deepens; Lord, with me abide:
When other helpers fail, and comforts flee,
Help of the helpless, O abide with me.

Swift to its close ebbs out life's little day;
Earth's joys grow dim, its glories pass away;
Change and decay in all around I see:
O thou who changest not, abide with me.

I need thy presence every passing hour;
What but thy grace can foil the tempter's power?
Who like thyself my guide and stay can be?
Through cloud and sunshine, Lord, abide with me.

I fear no foe with thee at hand to bless;
Ills have no weight, and tears no bitterness.
Where is death's sting? Where, grave, thy victory?
I triumph still, if thou abide with me.

Hold thou thy cross before my closing eyes;
Shine through the gloom, and point me to the skies;
Heaven's morning breaks, and earth's vain
   shadows flee;
In life, in death, O Lord, abide with me.

H. F. Lyte

I've only acted in Shakespeare once – as Juliet's Nurse, in a television production of *Romeo and Juliet*. The nurse was traditionally played as an old woman, and Dame Edith Evans and Dame Flora Robson had already made the role their own with their brilliant and deservedly famous interpretations.

The producer decided to make her someone younger, who could have been – as, really, she would have been – Juliet's wet nurse when she was a baby. I thoroughly enjoyed the experience. I don't know if I have been the only "wet-nursable" Nurse – but I think I can claim to have been the first!

I mention that – just "in passing" – because I wanted to tell, or perhaps remind, you that our Immortal Bard is believed by many scholars to have had a hand in the translation of what was to become the Authorized, the

King James' Version, of the Bible, in particular many of
the Psalms of David. When you read them, it's not
hard to believe that, is it?

Shakespeare also wrote prayers in many of his
plays. Here are one or two examples:

> O God, thy arm was here;
> And not to us, but to thy arm alone,
> Ascribe we all.
>
> > King Henry V – after Agincourt

> O Thou whose captain I account myself . . .
> To thee I do commend my watchful soul,
> Ere I let fall the windows of mine eyes;
> Sleeping or waking, O defend me still.
>
> > Henry, Earl of Richmond, before the
> > battle of Bosworth, in Richard III

> O Lord, that lends me life,
> Lend me a heart replete with thankfulness!
>
> > Henry VI part 2

Coming nearer to our own time, that old reprobate, the poet Dylan Thomas, wrote one of the most moving prayers in his radio masterpiece *Under Milk Wood*. Do you remember the sunset song of the Reverend Eli Jenkins?

> Every morning when I wake,
> Dear Lord, a little prayer I make,
> O please to keep Thy lovely eye
> On all poor creatures born to die.
>
> And every evening at sun-down
> I ask a blessing on the town,
> For whether we last the night or no
> I'm sure is always touch-and-go
>
> We are not wholly bad or good
> Who live our lives under Milk Wood,
> And Thou, I know, wilt be the first
> To see our best side, not our worst.
>
> O let us see another day!
> Bless us this night, I pray,
> And to the sun we all will bow
> And say, good-bye – but just for now!
>
> Dylan Thomas 1914–53

Really, you could write a whole book on the Prayers of the poets! I can't finish this chapter without including a few lines from John Betjeman, our late Poet Laureate, who was such a lovable man and is so much missed. His poems were often about the eccentricities of church people, and although I haven't found one that is really a prayer, I thought you'd enjoy the last few lines of *Blame the Vicar* – which is really like a benediction on us all!

Dear readers, from this rhyme take warning,
And if you heard the bell this morning
Your Vicar went to pray for you,
A task the Prayer Book bids him do.
"Highness" or "Lowness" do not matter,
You are the Church and must not scatter,
Cling to the Sacraments and pray
And God be with you every day.

John Betjeman
(in *Poems in the Porch*)

And there was delivered unto him the book of the prophet Esaias. And when he had opened the book, he found the place where it was written,

"The Spirit of the Lord is upon me, Because he hath anointed me to preach the gospel to the poor; He hath sent me to heal the brokenhearted, to preach deliverance to the captives, And recovering of sight to the blind, To set at liberty them that are bruised, To preach the acceptable year of the Lord.'
Luke 4:17–19 (AV)

Wordless Prayers

*

Lord of all pots and pans and things;
since I've no time to be a saint
by doing lovely things
or watching late with Thee,
or dreaming in the dawnlight
or storming heaven's gates,
make me a saint by getting meals,
and washing up the plates.

from *Short Prayers for the Long Day*

I just wanted to say in this chapter, as simply and briefly as I can, a little something about prayers that don't need to have any words at all.

Church bells ring out prayers and praise to the glory of the Lord every Sunday morning; they offer up the joy and happiness of a newly married couple on Saturdays; a muffled peal is a farewell prayer to an old friend, or the old year. And then the muffles are taken off and the bells give voice to faith in the resurrection.

Sometimes you might pass a church and hear a single bell chiming in a sequence – three rings, three rings, three rings, nine rings. Listen. That's the Angelus being rung, a reminder of the Angel Gabriel visiting Mary and telling her she was to be the mother of God's son. It's like a cue for everyone round about to pray together for a few moments.

The act of lighting a candle is a prayer. I don't just mean the formal candles on the altar. Many churches have those little iron stands, with spikes, in the side aisles, do you know the things I mean? Where you can fix and light your own little candles for people you want to pray for, to remember your dead, or even to be a sign of your own mission. Hindus have an annual Festival of Light called Diwali, where everyone puts lighted candles in their windows. It's a beautiful sight on a dark November night. Of course, you might merely be lighting a candle in your own home because of a power cut, or to enhance a romantic dinner – but bringing light into darkness is always a kind of prayer.

On Rogation Sunday many country congregations – especially when there are a lot of farmers among them – process out of their church at the end of the service, and going to the centre of their village, turn to face first north, then west, then south, then east, and ask for God's blessing on the crops and all the life of the community. So passers-by can see the prayers happening, even if they don't come close enough to catch the words.

During a Holy Communion service there is the moment they call "The Peace" when everyone shakes hands, or embraces, the people all around them, as a sign of Christian love and peace. If you don't know, and aren't expecting it, it can come as quite a shock to find yourself suddenly being seized in a big bear hug by a strange gentleman who up until then had been sitting looking very quiet and respectable beside you, probably reading his prayer book with his spectacles on the end of his nose!

A present can be a prayer – the person who receives it will remember and be thankful for the loving-kindness behind the gift every time they look at it. Oh – and that reminds me – another admission. Every time I dust at the cottage, I've got an owl sitting on a bit of fence, in pottery. I love it, but I've lost who it came from. The letter just got muddled into all the rest of the post somehow. So I was wondering, if you happen to be reading this, please would you write? You know, if it's only for me to write and thank you. Because it's beautiful.

Keeping your home warm and welcoming, arranging flowers in a vase – even if it's just sticking a few daffs in a milk-bottle – whatever is done with love, is a way of praying. Holding someone's hand, or lending them a hand with their chores are living prayers.

Praying is loving – loving God – and so almost any expression of love is a prayer.

> Seek Love in the pity of another's woe,
> In the gentle relief of another's care.
> In the darkness of night and the winter's snow,
> In the naked and outcast – seek love there.
>
> William Blake 1757–1827

Listening to someone, quietly and patiently and without interrupting or judging, while they pour their heart out to you, that's praying. Listening to God is the best kind of praying of all.

Teach us to listen, Lord
to one another with enjoyment
and especially:
to the diffident, with encouragement;
to the repetitive, with patience;
to the sad, with understanding;
to the happy, joyfully;
to the aggressive, calmly;
and to the gossip – never.
And above all, Lord
teach us to listen to you with our hearts.

"Listening" 1985 Clemency Greatorex

The kingdom of heaven is like yeast that a
woman took and mixed into a large amount
of flour until it worked all through the
dough. Matthew 13:33 (NIV)

Amen

*

May you be in heaven half an hour
before the Divil knows you're dead!

Irish blessing

Better by far that you should forget and smile,
Than that you should remember and be sad.

Christina Rossetti

Well, I'm all organized. We're going to have "O happy day" and "I'll go in the strength of the Lord" and – of course – my all-time favourite: "Onward Christian Soldiers". The Salvation Army have promised to come along with singers and a band, so if you happen to be passing the church, and hear the sound of great music and loud singing – you'll know it's only Thora, gone to her rest!

Not that I've got any plans to go just yet, I want you to understand. But "Be Prepared" is the watchword – well, it is when you're eighty years old! I want to make certain that it's going to be a great occasion – no tears, and plenty of rejoicing, and everyone having a great time. In fact I'm only sorry that I won't be there to join in!

Meanwhile I'm still enjoying life to the full, kindly note, and at the end I want to say, with Robert Louis Stevenson:

Under the wide and starry sky,
Dig the grave and let me die.
Glad did I live and gladly die,
And I laid me down with a will.

> Part of R. L. Stevenson's memorial plaque
> in St Giles Cathedral, Edinburgh

Here are some beautiful prayers, hymns and epitaphs,
bringers of comfort to the dying and the bereaved:

Here down my wearied limbs I'll lay;
My pilgrim's staff; my weed of gray;
My palmer's hat; my scallop shell;
My cross; my cord; and all farewell.

> Robert Herrick (1591–1674)

God be in my head,
And in my understanding
God be in my eyes,
And in my looking;
God be in my mouth,
And in my speaking;
God be in my heart,
And in my thinking;
God be at my end,
And at my departing.

> Sarum Missal

My Master said: "Trust!" –
So I must
Abide here quite still
Awaiting His will . . .
Until, on a day,
Shall I hear Him say
"Paid for!" and then? –
"Alleluia! Amen!"

Sister Maud CAH
Tailwags No. 3

Death be not proud, though some have called thee
Mighty and dreadful, for thou art not so,
For those whom thou think'st thou doest overthrow,
Die not, poor death, nor yet canst thou kill me.
From rest and sleep, which but thy pictures be,
Much pleasure, then from thee much more must flow,
And soonest our best men with thee do go,
Rest of their bones and soul's delivery . . .

One short sleep past, we wake eternally,
And death shall be no more; death, thou shalt die.

John Donne (1572–1631)

Deep peace of the running wave to you.
Deep peace of the flowing air to you.
Deep peace of the quiet earth to you.
Deep peace of the shining stars to you.
Deep peace of the Son of Peace to you.

Celtic Benediction

Death is nothing at all. I have only slipped away into the next room. I am I, and you are you, whatever we were to each other, that we are still.

Call me by my old familiar name. Speak to me in the easy way which we always used. Put no difference into your tone; wear no forced air of solemnity or sorrow. Laugh as we always laughed at the little jokes we enjoyed together. Play, smile, think of me, pray for me.

Let my name be ever the household word that it always was. Let it be spoken without an effort, without the trace of a shadow in it.

Life means all that it ever meant; it is the same as it ever was; there is absolutely unbroken continuity.

What is this death, but a negligible accident? Why should I be out of mind because I am out of sight? I am but waiting for you, for an interval, somewhere very near, just around the corner. All is well.

Canon Henry Scott Holland (1847–1918)

Lord, now lettest thou thy servant depart in peace,
According to thy word:
For mine eyes have seen thy salvation,
Which thou hast prepared before the face of all people;
A light to lighten the Gentiles,
And the glory of thy people Israel.

Luke 2:29–32 (AV)

And God shall wipe away all tears from their eyes; and there shall be no more death, neither sorrow, nor crying, neither shall there be any more pain: for the former things are passed away.

Revelation 21:4 (AV)

Lo, Jesus meets us, risen from the tomb;
Lovingly he greets us, scatters fear and gloom;
Let the Church with gladness hymns of triumph sing,
For her Lord now liveth, death hath lost its sting:

Thine be the glory, risen, conquering Son,
Endless is the victory thou o'er death hast won.

E. L. Budry (1854–1932)
tr. R. B. Hoyle (1875–1939)

Father, into thy hands I commend my spirit.

Luke 23:46 (AV)

The Grace

✳

I like to think that God will spare me to be here in his wonderful world a litle longer, enabling me to finish this little book on a more cheerful note!

When one is surrounded with love, as I am, life *is* wonderful, isn't it?

The grace of our Lord, Jesus Christ,
and the love of God,
and the fellowship of the Holy Spirit
be with us all evermore

Amen
(based on 2 Corinthians 13·14)

✳

Acknowledgements

*

Whilst most of the items quoted in this book are no longer in copyright, the authors gratefully acknowledge use of the following items:

"Blame the Vicar" from *Poems in the Porch* by John Betjeman, published by Faber & Faber.

"Listening" and "Martha's Prayer" by Clemency Greatorex (unpublished).

Various extracts from the New International Version of the Bible (NIV), copyright © 1978 New York International Bible Society, published in Great Britain by Hodder and Stoughton.

—